BROOKLYN BOOK BODEGA

BLACK HISTORY
Biographies

Martin Luther King Jr.

Izzi Howell

CRABTREE
PUBLISHING COMPANY
WWW.CRABTREEBOOKS.COM

CRABTREE
PUBLISHING COMPANY
WWW.CRABTREEBOOKS.COM

Published in Canada
Crabtree Publishing
616 Welland Ave.
St. Catharines, Ontario
L2M 5V6

Published in the United States
Crabtree Publishing
347 Fifth Avenue
Suite 1402–145
New York, NY 10016

All words in **bold** appear in the glossary on page 23.

Published in 2021 by Crabtree Publishing Company

First published by The Watts Publishing Group
Copyright © The Watts Publishing Group, 2019

Author: Izzi Howell

Editorial director: Kathy Middleton

Series editor: Izzi Howell

Editor: Ellen Rodger

Series designer: Rocket Design Ltd

Designer: Clare Nicholas

Proofreader: Crystal Sikkens

**Production coordinator and
  Prepress technician:** Ken Wright

Print coordinator: Katherine Berti

Literacy consultant: Kate Ruttle

The publisher would like to thank the following for permission to reproduce their pictures: Alamy: Everett Collection Historical 12, Everett Collection Inc 16; Getty: Hulton-Deutsch Collection/Corbis cover, Francis Miller/The LIFE Picture Collection 4, Bettmann 5, 9, 14 and 15, George Tames/New York Times Co. 7, Donald Uhrbrock/The LIFE Images Collection 10, Robert W. Kelley/The LIFE Picture Collection 11, Grey Villet/The LIFE Picture Collection 13, Lynn Pelham/The LIFE Picture Collection 18, Kirkikis 19; Shutterstock: Uncle Leo title page, alisafarov 6, Everett Historical 8, Joseph Sohm 17, Katherine Welles 20, Katherine Welles 21t; Wikimedia: Hpeterswald 21b.

Every attempt has been made to clear copyright. Should there be any inadvertent omission please apply to the publisher for rectification.

Printed in Canada/032021/CPC20210303

Library and Achives Canada Cataloguing in Publication

Title: Martin Luther King Jr. / Izzi Howell.
Names: Howell, Izzi, author.
Description: Series statement: Black history biographies | Originally published: London: Franklin Watts, 2019. | Includes index.
Identifiers: Canadiana (print) 20200358537 |
  Canadiana (ebook) 20200358545 |
  ISBN 9781427127907 (hardcover) |
  ISBN 9781427127969 (softcover) |
  ISBN 9781427128027 (HTML)
Subjects: LCSH: King, Martin Luther, Jr., 1929-1968—Juvenile literature. | LCSH: African American civil rights workers—United States—Biography—Juvenile literature.
Classification: LCC E187.97.K5 H69 2021 | DDC j323.092—dc23

Library of Congress Cataloging-in-Publication Data

Names: Howell, Izzi, author.
Title: Martin Luther King, Jr. / Izzi Howell.
Description: New York, NY : Crabtree Publishing Company, 2021. | Series: Black history biographies | Includes index.
Identifiers: LCCN 2020045868 (print) | LCCN 2020045869 (ebook) |
  ISBN 9781427127907 (hardcover) |
  ISBN 9781427127969 (paperback) |
  ISBN 9781427128027 (ebook)
Subjects: LCSH: King, Martin Luther, Jr., 1929-1968--Juvenile literature. | African Americans--Biography--Juvenile literature. | Civil rights workers--United States--Biography--Juvenile literature. | African Americans--Civil rights--History--20th century--Juvenile literature.
Classification: LCC E185.97.K5 H595 2021 (print) |
  LCC E185.97.K5 (ebook) | DDC 323.092 [B]--dc23
LC record available at https://lccn.loc.gov/2020045868
LC ebook record available at https://lccn.loc.gov/2020045869

Contents

Martin Luther King Jr.

Dr. Martin Luther King Jr. was an American **activist** who fought against **racism**. He was an important person in the **Civil Rights Movement**.

Martin Luther King Jr. made important **speeches** in front of many people. ▼

A lot of people walked with Martin Luther King Jr. in marches. ▶

Martin Luther King Jr.

Do you know anyone who has been on a march? What was the march about?

Martin Luther King Jr. helped Black people get the same **rights** as White people in the United States.

Childhood

Martin Luther King Jr. was born on January 15, 1929. He lived with his family in the city of Atlanta, Georgia.

Atlanta

King lived with his parents and his brother and sister in this large house in Atlanta. ▼

DR. KING'S BIRTHPLACE 10:00-12:00 OPEN HOUSE TOURS NO NEED TO REGISTER

King went to university when he was 15. At university, he decided to become a **pastor**. He earned many **degrees** at university, including the highest, a PhD.

King worked as a pastor after he finished university. ▶

Black people and White people

For many years, Black people and White people were **segregated** in America. They lived in different areas, went to different schools, and ate in different places.

◀ This theater was for Black people. Many places did not allow Black people at all.

In the past, the word colored was used to describe Black people.

Over time and with effort, **laws** changed. Black people could share spaces with White people. This made some White people unhappy.

▲ Black students were met with racism and hatred when they tried to go to school with White students.

Civil rights

In the early 1900s, groups started working to make things fairer for Black people. By the 1950s, **protests** pushed for change. This was the beginning of the Civil Rights Movement.

Martin Luther King Jr. met with other people to organize protests. ▼

Martin Luther King Jr. wanted to protest **peacefully**. He thought this was the best way to change things.

▲
Marching with signs was one way that King protested peacefully.

Protests

In 1955, a Black woman named Rosa Parks was arrested because she refused to give her seat on the bus to a White man. In the area where Parks lived, Black people could only sit at the back of the bus.

Rosa Parks was taken to the police station after she was arrested.
▶

How would you feel if you could only sit in a certain part of the bus?

▲
During the bus boycott, Black people walked to work instead of taking the bus.

Civil rights groups decided to protest. Martin Luther King Jr. helped to organize a bus **boycott** in the town. Black people stopped taking the bus. After a year, the law was changed so Black people could sit anywhere on the bus.

The March on Washington

In 1963, King helped to organize a huge march. Around 250,000 people walked through the city of Washington, D.C., the nation's capital.

▼ People on the march carried signs asking for civil rights and better jobs for Black people.

After the march, King gave a speech to the marchers. In the speech, he talked about his dream of Black and White people being treated the same.

King's famous speech is known as the "I Have a Dream" speech. ▼

New rights

Civil rights protests showed everyone that Black people were being treated unfairly. After years of these protests, a new law was passed in 1964. The law said that Black and White people had to be treated the same.

King stood behind President Lyndon B. Johnson when Johnson signed the new law. ▼

The new law made things better for Black people in the U.S.A. However, many Black people are still treated **unequally** in America and many other countries around the world.

These people are taking part in a march. They are angry that Black people are still treated unfairly.
▼

Death

On April 4, 1968, Martin Luther King Jr. was shot and killed. Everyone was very shocked. He was only 39 years old.

◀ Thousands of people walked through the streets at King's funeral.

Martin Luther King Jr. is buried in Atlanta. His wife Coretta was buried with him after she died in 2006.

People lay wreaths on King's grave to show respect. ▼

REV. MARTIN LUTHER KING, JR.
1929 – 1968
"Free at last, Free at last,
Thank God Almighty
I'm Free at last."

CORETTA SCOTT KING
1927 – 2006
"And now abide Faith, Hope,
Love, These Three; but the
greatest of these is Love."
1 Cor. 13:13

The word "Rev." means "reverend," another word for pastor.

Remembering

The life and work of Martin Luther King Jr. is remembered in many ways. Throughout America, people celebrate Martin Luther King Jr. Day in January.

▲ Streets in some U.S. cities are named after Martin Luther King Jr.

There are statues and murals of Martin Luther King Jr. around the world.

This statue is at Westminster Abbey in London, U.K.▶

This mural was painted in Sydney, Australia. It celebrates King's famous "I Have a Dream" speech.▼

How can you help to fight against racism, like Dr. King?

"I have a dream"

www.dharug.dalang.com

Quiz

Test how much you remember.

Check your answers on page 24.

1 When was Martin Luther King Jr. born?

2 Name one way that King protested peacefully.

3 Who was Rosa Parks?

4 Where did King organize a march in 1963?

5 When did King die?

6 Name one way that King is remembered today.

Glossary

activist Someone who tries to change society

boycott When people stop doing or using something as a way of protesting

Civil Rights Movement A struggle for fairness and justice for Black Americans in the 1950s and 1960s

degrees Certificates awarded to students for finishing their studies at university

laws Rules in a country

marches Organized walks by groups to show they do not agree with something

pastor A leader in a church

peacefully Calmly and without violence

president The leader of a government

protests Acts that show you disagree with something

racism Treating people badly because of their race or the color of their skin

rights The things you can do or have, according to the laws of your country

segregated Separated or set apart from others

signed To have written your name on something to show you agree with it

speeches Talks given by a person to groups of people

unequally When something is done unfairly

Index

Answers:

1: January 15, 1929; 2: Marching with signs; 3: A woman who was arrested because she refused to give her seat on the bus to a White man; 4: Washington, D.C.; 5: April 4, 1968; 6: Celebrating Martin Luther King Jr. Day, on street signs, with statues

Teaching notes:

Some children should be able to enjoy this book as independent readers. Other children will need more support.

Before you share the book:

- Ask what do readers already know about the Civil Rights Movement in the 1950s and 60s?
- Introduce the idea of segregation and different laws for different people based on race. Do the children think this sounds like a fair system?

While you share the book:

- Help children to read some of the more unfamiliar words.

- Talk about the questions. Encourage children to make links between their own experiences and the events described.
- Talk about the pictures. How can you tell that some of the pictures were taken a long time ago?

After you have shared the book:

- Talk about ways of protesting if you think things are unfair. Discuss why Martin Luther King Jr. might have decided that peaceful protests, such as marches, were better than other actions.
- Ask children what they think people today should learn from Martin Luther King Jr.